·TELL ME ABOUT·
THE WORLD OF ANIMALS

By Tom Stacy
Illustrated by Eric Robson

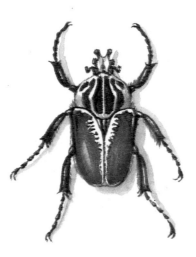

WARWICK PRESS

Published in 1991 by Warwick Press,
387 Park Avenue South, New York, N.Y. 10016.
First published in 1990 by Kingfisher Books.
Copyright © 1990 Grisewood & Dempsey Ltd.

Printed in Spain
ISBN 0-531-19103-6

Contents

What are animals like?

There are thousands of different animals in the world, but they all have one thing in common. They have to move around in order to find food and water. Unlike plants, animals cannot stay in one place and remain alive. Some animals look for plants to eat; others hunt and kill other animals. But whether they have legs, wings, or fins, animals have to search for food.

In the northern forests, owls fly silently at night, hunting small animals to eat.

Forest deer graze on grass, bark, and leaves. Only male deer have antlers.

The stealthy lynx hunts small animals. Like all cats, it has very keen eyesight.

Bears catch fish in the rivers. On land they also look for fruit and berries to eat.

The otter lives in a riverbank den. It can swim fast, which helps it to catch fish.

Woodpeckers use their powerful beaks to drill into tree bark in search of insects.

The porcupine chews pine tree bark. Its spiny quills protect it from enemies.

The squirrel uses its sharp teeth to gnaw nuts. It buries some food for winter.

Raccoons eat crabs, frogs, fish, birds' eggs, insects, plants – almost anything!

ANIMAL FACTS

• The animal world is divided into two main groups – vertebrates and invertebrates. Vertebrates are animals with backbones. They range in size from elephants and tigers to rabbits and mice.

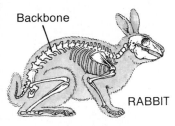

Backbone

RABBIT

• Invertebrates are animals that don't have backbones – insects such as flies, as well as worms and jellyfish.

JELLYFISH

• Experts have named nearly 1.3 million animals. Around 96% are invertebrates. Just 4% are vertebrates.

• There are five main vertebrate groups – fish, amphibians, reptiles, birds, and mammals.

• There are around 21,500 species, or types, of fish.

• Amphibians can live on land and in water. There are over 4,000 species, and they include frogs and toads.

• Snakes, lizards, and crocodiles are all reptiles. There are over 6,500 species, and most live on land.

• There are around 8,800 bird species, of all shapes, sizes, and colors.

• Mammals are the only animals whose young feed on the mother's milk. Familiar animals such as cats belong to this group, as well as lions and bears. There are over 4,000 species.

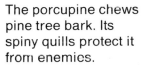

Where do animals live?

Animals live in every part of Earth – on land, in the ocean, and in the air. The area surrounding an animal's home is called its habitat. There are different habitats all over our planet, with different kinds of animals living in each one.

GREENLAND

NORTH AMERICA

Animals of the icy north, such as polar bears, have thick coats or layers of fat to keep them warm.

AFRICA

Some animals of the prairies graze on its short grasses. Some hunt and kill other animals for their food.

SOUTH AMERICA

Rain forests are hot and wet. Many animals sleep in the day and hunt in the cool of the night.

Deserts are hot and very dry. Camels and other desert animals have to survive with little or no water to drink.

Shy animals like badgers, owls, and deer live hidden in the cool dark forests of the United States.

Animals have all kinds of ways of surviving the different habitats in which they live. Desert animals have to manage with very little water, for example. Some never drink; they get all the water they need from their food instead. Others can live for long periods of time on the water stored in their body fat.

EUROPE

The deep oceans are rich in animal life of all shapes and sizes, from jellyfish to octopuses and sharks.

ASIA

Australia is home to unusual animals such as the emu, the kangaroo, the platypus, and the koala

AUSTRALIA

Lions are the big hunters of the African plains. The rhinoceros and the antelope are grass eaters.

The icy coastal waters of Antarctica are the habitat of seals and whales, as well as penguins and other seabirds.

ANTARCTICA

Which animal lives the longest?

The longest living animals are tortoises — some live to be over 150 years old! Because they face many dangers, wild animals don't usually live as long as pets or zoo animals. And, as a rule, big animals live longer than small ones like insects.

Adult mayflies live for only a few hours.

Houseflies live for about 2 weeks.

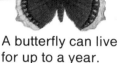

A butterfly can live for up to a year.

A mouse may live as long as 5 years.

Hamsters can live for 10 years.

A dog is very old at 15 years.

Horses can live to be 40 years old.

Cockatoos live for as long as 75 years.

Some giant tortoises live to be over 150.

SNAIL WATCHING

Snails live for 2 to 3 years, but you needn't spend that long watching them! Mark a snail's shell with a felt-tip pen (it won't hurt the snail). See where it goes and what it eats.

Which is the cleverest animal?

Animal intelligence is hard to measure, but most experts think that chimpanzees and dolphins are at the head of the class. Chimpanzees can use simple tools, and dolphins talk to one another underwater, using a musical language of their own.

Chimpanzees use sticks as tools to "fish" termites from their nests. Dolphins are playful and can easily be trained to perform tricks.

Which is the most dangerous animal?

Although a few types of shark will attack swimmers, the deadliest animals arc smaller. Some snakes, spiders, and jellyfish have poisonous bites or stings which can kill a person in minutes. The frog shown below has enough poison to kill 500 people!

? DO YOU KNOW

As many as 40,000 people a year are killed as a result of snake bites. Most deaths are caused by the Indian cobra.

The little golden arrow-poison frog is even more deadly than the great white shark.

The saw-edged teeth of the great white shark can be 3 inches long.

What are the fastest animals?

DO YOU KNOW

The slowest mammal is the three-toed sloth. It sleeps for 16 hours out of every 24, and takes a whole day to travel just 300 feet!

Birds are the recordholders for speed. In a dive, a peregrine falcon can reach 215 miles per hour (mph) – only the fastest racecar could beat it! In level flight another bird, the Asian spine-tailed swift, can fly at speeds of more than 100 mph. The champion sprinter of all the land animals is the cheetah. But in a race it would just be beaten by a fish – the sailfish.

| mph | 0.6 | 6 | 12 | 18 | 25 | 31 | 37 | 44 |

The champion long-distance traveler is a seabird called the Arctic tern. It nests in the Arctic, near the North Pole. When summer ends there, it flies to the South Pole, where summer is just beginning. Each year the amazing Arctic tern travels up to 23,000 miles on its round trip across the world!

SPEED FACTS

	mph
Spine-tailed swift	100+
Sailfish	68
Cheetah	62+
Racing pigeon	60+
Pronghorn	60
Dragonfly	49
Gazelle	49
Hare	45
Racehorse	44
Ostrich	39
Greyhound	39
Fox	39
Zebra	39
Shark	39
Kangaroo	39
Lion	36
Giraffe	32
Cat	29
Elephant	25
Sea lion	25
Dolphin	25
Human	20
Bat	15
Pig	11
Honeybee	11
Chicken	8
Housefly	5
Goldfish	4
Snake	2
Spider	1
Tortoise	0.25
Sloth	0.06
Snail	0.03

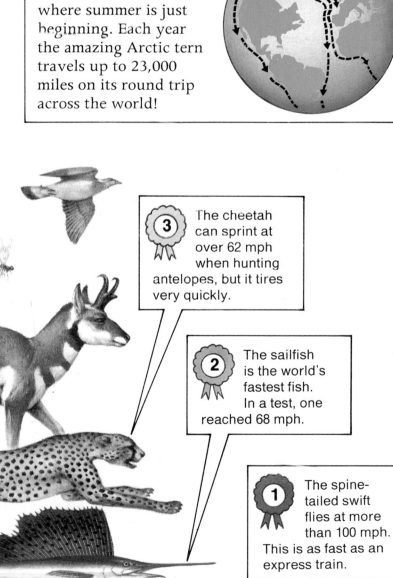

3 The cheetah can sprint at over 62 mph when hunting antelopes, but it tires very quickly.

2 The sailfish is the world's fastest fish. In a test, one reached 68 mph.

1 The spine-tailed swift flies at more than 100 mph. This is as fast as an express train.

| 49 | 56 | 62 | 68 | 75 | 80 | 87 | 93 | 100 |

What are the largest animals?

Whales are the largest animals on Earth. And the biggest whale is the blue whale, which can be 100 feet long and weigh as much as 165 tons. The largest land animal is the African elephant, which is twice as tall as a person and can weigh $6\frac{1}{2}$ tons.

 DO YOU KNOW

Some animals are called Goliath after a giant in the Bible. The Goliath beetle below is as heavy as an apple. The Goliath spider is as big as this page!

The tallest animal is the giraffe (18 feet). African elephants are the heaviest plant eaters (6 tons), while the largest meat eater is the Kodiak bear (10 feet). The ostrich is the biggest bird (8 feet high). The longest snake is the reticulated python (33 feet).

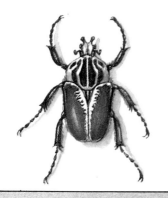

The blue whale is not a fish, but a mammal – its young feed on their mother's milk.

DO YOU KNOW

It would take about 25 African elephants (each weighing 6½ tons) to balance the weight of just one blue whale! Even though the blue whale can weigh a staggering 165 tons, it lives on tiny shrimps called krill, which are only about 2 inches long. A blue whale may eat as much as 2 or 3 tons of krill in one meal.

The giant squid can be 65 feet long from its tentacles to the tip of its body.

The largest fish is the harmless whale shark. It grows to 50 feet long.

Why do elephants have trunks?

As well as a nose to breathe through, an elephant's trunk is a hand for picking things up. It's long enough to reach up into treetops for leaves, or down into pools for water. An elephant can even use its trunk like a hose to spray itself with water.

DO YOU KNOW

The African elephant is bigger than the Asian elephant. Its ears are larger too. Its trunk ends in two lobes, not one.

African has two lobes

Asian has one lobe

AFRICAN

ASIAN

Large ears

Small ears

Why are giraffes' necks so long?

With its long neck, a giraffe can reach even higher than an elephant's trunk to eat the juiciest leaves at the tops of trees.

The giraffe's extra-long neck has just seven bones – the same number as we have in ours!

DO YOU KNOW

The giraffe can't bend its neck. To drink, it spreads its legs and lowers its head.

Why do camels have humps?

A camel's hump helps it to survive life in the desert, where food and water are often scarce. When a camel has plenty to eat, its hump becomes firm with extra fat. The camel can then go without food or water for weeks, living off the emergency supplies in its hump.

DO YOU KNOW

There are two kinds of camel. The dromedary has just one hump. The Bactrian camel of central Asia has two humps.

Why do zebras have stripes?

No one knows why zebras have stripes. The stripes may make it easier for zebras to see each other and stay together. They might also help to confuse enemies, making it difficult to pick out a single zebra from a galloping herd.

DO YOU KNOW

A tiger's stripes help it to hide by blending into the shadows and long grasses.

Why do animals hibernate?

Hibernation is like a deep sleep, which some animals go into when food is scarce. In late summer, for example, the dormouse crams itself with fruit and nuts until it is very fat. Then it curls up inside its nest and goes to sleep. The dormouse lives off its body fat throughout the winter and wakes up in spring – thin and very hungry!

DO YOU KNOW

One type of Australian desert frog only comes out of hibernation after rain. It then lays its eggs in shallow pools, and its young grow into frogs before the pools dry out. Then each frog burrows into the sand, wrapping itself in a see-through skin to keep in body water. It may wait 2 years for the next rain.

Many hibernators are insect eaters, like the hedgehog in its nest of dead leaves.

Snakes become sluggish in cold weather. They begin to stir only when it gets warmer.

Bats cluster together for winter, sleeping upside down in caves and old buildings.

Bears don't sleep deeply all winter. They wake on warm days to look for food to eat.

Chipmunks store food in their burrows. They wake on warm winter days to eat from their supplies.

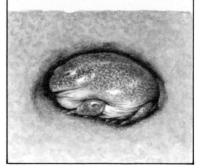

The dormouse sleeps soundly in its nest until spring brings fresh plant food for it to eat.

Why do kangaroos have pouches?

A kangaroo mother protects her baby in her pouch for the first few months of its life. A baby kangaroo is the size of a bumblebee when it crawls into the pouch. It stays there, feeding on its mother's milk, until it is big enough to survive in the world outside. Animals that raise their young in pouches are called marsupials.

Kangaroos spring along on their big, powerful hind legs. Their long tails help them to balance.

MARSUPIAL FACTS

● There are about 270 marsupial species. The Americas are home to about 90.

● Australia has 180 or so types of marsupial, including kangaroos, koalas, and wombats.

NATURE DETECTIVE

Look for clues to show that animals have been feeding nearby. Look at nuts for animals' tooth marks, for example, and see if you can find any trees stripped of their bark by animals such as grazing deer.

Nut by mouse   Cone by squirrel   Bark by deer

Why do chameleons change color?

Chameleons are a type of lizard whose skin color changes with their mood – an angry chameleon will turn black! Chameleons are also affected by light and temperature, and their skin changes slowly to match the colors of their surroundings.

LIZARD FACTS

● The largest lizard is Indonesia's Komodo dragon (10 feet).

● The tuatara of New Zealand (below) can live to be over 100 years old.

Why do lizards lose their tails?

Most lizards can shed their tails when they want to. They often do this to escape enemies, who are left clutching a wriggling bit of tail while the lizard escapes! The lizard's tail grows back again, but it is slightly shorter than before.

The hawk is left with only a wriggling tail in its talons, while the lizard escapes to grow a new tail.

Animals like hawks, which hunt and kill other animals for food, are called predators.

Why do animals have shells?

All sorts of animals have shells, from crabs and lobsters to tortoises and turtles. Most of them have soft bodies, and their shells act like armor, protecting them from enemies. A tortoise, for example, can hide inside its shell if danger threatens.

DO YOU KNOW

Tortoises (left) are land animals. Turtles (below) live in water and have paddle-like legs for swimming. Their shells are flatter than those of tortoises.

How do crocodiles hunt?

A crocodile will often lie in wait for animals that come to drink at the river's edge. It floats like a log, showing only its eyes and nostrils above water. If an animal strays too close, the crocodile grabs it and drags it underwater until it drowns.

DO YOU KNOW

Crocodiles have narrower jaws than alligators, and the fourth tooth in a crocodile's lower jaw sticks out.

Alligator

Crocodile

How do birds fly?

Birds have two ways of flying – they glide with their wings outstretched, or they flap their wings up and down. Some birds use both methods. Small birds beat their wings very fast; large birds tend to make slow wingbeats.

Birds have light bones and powerful muscles to help them fly. Their feathers keep them warm and make a smooth surface for the air to flow over in flight.

The frigate bird (below) has long pointed wings and a forked tail. It is a superb flier.

On broad wings over 10 feet across, the condor (above) soars on warm air currents above the mountains.

MAKE A BIRD MOBILE

1 Draw a body and two wings for each bird on cardboard. Color them and cut them out (ask an adult to help you). Now fold the ends of each wing and staple them to the bodies.

2 With an adult's help, make a frame from two wire coat hangers.

3 Weight each bird with modeling clay. Tie the finished birds to the frame. Use different lengths of string so the hanging birds don't bump into each other.

Fold wing and staple to body

The kestrel (left) hovers as it hunts. Wings beating and tail spread, it waits in the sky.

The albatross (above) is a glidor, with the biggest wingspan of all birds – nearly 13 feet across!

The fastest fliers are the swifts (left). Their wings are swept back, like the wings of jet planes.

DO YOU KNOW

Not all birds can fly. Flightless birds include the largest living birds – the ostrich and the emu. Kiwis are shy flightless birds which live in New Zealand. They wander around at night, hunting for a juicy meal of insects and worms.

Penguins can't fly, but they can swim well. They use their wings as flippers in the water.

Emu

Kiwi

Emperor penguins

How do bats fly?

Bats fly by flapping their wings, just like birds do. Bats are mammals, however, not birds. Bats don't have feathers, and their wings are covered with skin. A bat's wings are like a tent of thin skin which stretches from the tips of the bat's fingerbones down to its feet and across to its tail.

Bats sleep during the day, roosting upside down in trees and caves. They wake at dusk.

Most bats see quite well, but their large ears help them to track insects when hunting at night.

 BAT FACTS

- The biggest bats are called flying foxes. Their wings can be 5 feet across.

- The smallest bat is Kitti's hog-nosed bat – it's no bigger than a bumblebee.

 **DO YOU KNOW**

Some bats find insects in the dark by echo-location – sending out a stream of noise and measuring how far away an insect is by the time it takes the noise to reach the insect and bounce off its body.

Bat sends out high-pitched squeaks

Echo bounces off insect

Can fish fly?

Fish can't really fly, but some can glide above the water to escape their enemies. Flying fish have extralong shoulder fins which spread like wings. Once airborne, they can glide for more than 300 feet.

Can frogs fly?

Tree frogs are expert climbers, and some species will leap into the air to catch insects to eat. Some tree frogs have large webbed feet which work like parachutes. If they leap from a tree, they can glide for about 40 feet.

Tree frogs have pads on their fingers and toes which help them to climb trees.

How do fish swim?

Fish swim by waving or rippling their bodies along. The fish tightens the muscles down the side of its body – one side after the other – and this makes it ripple through the water. Its tail also helps, by pushing against the water behind it.

The fin on top of a fish's back is called its dorsal fin. The fish uses this fin to help it change direction.

The tail wiggles from side to side, helping to push the fish through the water.

The fish uses these fins – its pectoral fins – to keep its balance as it swims along.

To swim, the fish tightens the muscles down each side of its body – one side after the other. This sets up a rippling movement which pushes the fish through the water.

 DO YOU KNOW

The sea horse swims slowly in an upright position by fanning its small dorsal fin so quickly that it looks like a boat's propeller.

MAKE AN AQUARIUM

1 You'll need a fish tank or a large glass container. With a grownup's help, put in a layer of washed gravel and fill the tank slowly with clean water.

2 Plant some water-weed and add a broken flowerpot for your fish to hide in.

3 Let the tank stand for 3 days before you put in the fish. Don't over-crowd them – one small fish needs as much as 4 quarts of water.

How do fish breathe underwater?

All animals need to breathe oxygen to live. Unlike land animals, which take oxygen from the air, fish take it from the water in which they live. Inside a fish's body is a special part called the gills, which take oxygen from the water.

To breathe, a fish gulps in water and passes it through its gills, where oxygen is absorbed into its bloodstream.

Hundreds of different colorful fish live in the warm, shallow waters around coral reefs.

Grouper

Shark

Clown triggerfish

Neon gobies

Blue trunkfish

Moorish idols

Blue-striped grunt

Long-spine squirrelfish

Clown-fish

Long-snouted coral fish

Trumpet-fish

Moray eel

? DO YOU KNOW

Mudskippers are fish which can breathe oxygen from air as well as from water. On land, they use their pectoral fins to help them balance. They get around by wriggling and jumping!

Are all snakes poisonous?

Few snakes are poisonous. Some snakes kill animals for food by crushing them in their jaws. Others coil their long bodies around their victims and squeeze them to death. Of nearly 2,400 different snake species, only 300 or so use the needle-sharp fangs in their jaws to inject a deadly poison.

The reticulated python (below) – all pythons squeeze their victims to death.

The Australian taipan (below) is one of the world's most poisonous snakes.

SNAKE FACTS

• Snakes can swallow animals wider than themselves. They open their mouths very wide by un-hinging their jaws.

• The reticulated python grows to 33 feet and is the world's longest snake. It uses its powerful body to squeeze its victims to death, and it can even kill pigs and deer.

• Vipers have the longest poison fangs of all snakes – some have fangs 2 inches long!

The king cobra (left) rears up when frightened. All cobras have poison fangs.

Anacondas (below) rarely go far from water. They drown their victims or squeeze them to death.

Rattlesnakes (right) are very poisonous. They rattle the ends of their tails as a warning signal.

How do snakes move?

Even though they don't have legs, some snakes can move quicker than you can walk. Snakes have very strong muscles which they can tighten and relax to ripple or throw their bodies along. Some also dig the broad scales beneath their bodies into the ground and then push against these "anchors."

1 Most snakes use their muscular bodies to ripple over stony ground, pushing against stones and other objects.

2 Most sidewinding snakes live in deserts. To move, this snake anchors its head and tail, then flings its middle sideways.

3 On smoother ground a snake may concertina its body, anchor its tail, then throw its head forward.

DO YOU KNOW

Snakes are expert hunters, even though they don't see or hear well. They hunt mainly by smell, and they can use their tongues to taste the air and ground while tracking a victim by its scent. Some snakes also have special heat sensors and can sense the exact position of an animal by the body heat it gives off.

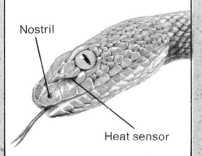

Nostril

Heat sensor

1

2

3

How do tadpoles become frogs?

Tadpoles are more like tiny fish than frogs. They live in water, where they swim around breathing through gills. Tadpoles develop legs as they change into frogs, however. They also lose their gills and grow lungs for breathing on land.

1 Frogs lay jelly-like clumps of spawn, or eggs, in water.

4 Then they grow two front legs. Their tails shrink away, and they develop lungs.

2 Each egg grows into a tiny tadpole, which breathes through gills.

3 After a few weeks the tadpoles grow two back legs.

TADPOLE WATCHING

1 See for yourself how tadpoles grow into frogs! Collect a little frog spawn from a pond in spring.

2 Put it in a bowl with some pond water and weed. Start a diary to record all the changes as they take place.

3 You should see some tiny tadpoles after about 10 days. They'll get their food from the weed at first. When their legs begin to grow, give your tadpoles fish food to eat.

4 When all their legs have grown, put a stone in the bowl so the froglets can hop out of the water to breathe air.

5 When they lose their tails, it's time to take your baby frogs back to their pond.

DO YOU KNOW

Animals which live on land and in water are called amphibians. Even though most adult amphibians have lungs for breathing on land, they can't live far from water. This is because their skin is slimy and has to be kept fairly damp.

How can you tell frogs from toads?

There's very little difference between most frogs and toads, and it's often difficult to tell them apart. However, frogs tend to hop and leap about on land, while toads generally have shorter back legs and prefer to crawl. Frogs usually have smooth skin, while a toad's skin is warty.

DO YOU KNOW

The record for a frog leap is over 21 feet, by a bullfrog.

AMPHIBIAN FACTS

• The Goliath frog of Africa is the world's largest frog. It can grow to 14 inches – that's nearly the width of two spread pages of this book – and weigh 6½ pounds!

• The largest amphibians are the giant salamanders of China and Japan. They sometimes grow to be more than 5 feet from head to tail tip.

• Unlike frogs and toads, salamanders (below) never lose their tails. They have small legs and move on land with short, clumsy steps.

Male frogs (right) blow up their throats with air when calling to attract a mate.

Most toads (below) have warty skin. The warts of some toads can be poisonous.

How do caterpillars become butterflies?

? DO YOU KNOW

Moths are related to butterflies. You can tell the difference between them by their wings. Butterflies fold their wings over their backs when resting. Moths spread theirs out flat.

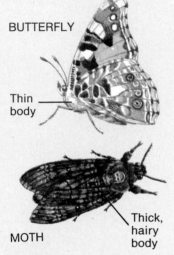

BUTTERFLY

Thin body

Thick, hairy body

MOTH

WATCHING BUTTERFLIES

Learn about butterflies by watching them, not catching them. In summer, look for different kinds of butterfly. See which flowers they feed on, and look on leaves for eggs and caterpillars. Find out which garden flowers attract butterflies, and see if you can grow some.

Every butterfly goes through four very different stages in its life cycle. It starts as an egg, which then hatches into a caterpillar. Next it turns into a pupa, after which it finally becomes an adult. This life cycle can take a few weeks or several years.

1 The life cycle of a butterfly begins when a female lays her eggs on a plant. A hungry caterpillar hatches from each egg.

2 The caterpillar spends most of its time eating. It crawls around, chewing on leaves, and grows quickly.

4 The adult butterfly forms inside the pupa. When it is ready, it splits the pupa case open and crawls out.

3 When the caterpillar is fully grown, it turns into a pupa. It doesn't eat, and it looks dead.

BUTTERFLY & MOTH FACTS

● The biggest butter-flies are the birdwings of Southeast Asia (below), with wing-spans of 10 inches. Measure this against your hands!

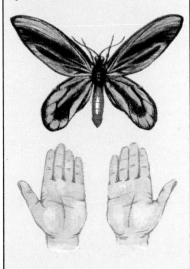

● The largest moth is the ghost moth (below) from Central and South America. It measures more than 11 inches across.

● Other giant moths are the Atlas moth of India and the Hercules moth of Australia. Both measure about 10 inches across.

How do spiders spin webs?

Spiders spin their webs with two kinds of silk, which they make inside their bodies. One is a tough silk for the web's frame. The other is stretchy and sticky, and is used by the spider to weave its main insect trap.

1 The spider begins by spinning a bridge of tough silk, which it makes inside its body.

2 Then it pulls down a thread to make a triangle shape.

3 It adds more tough threads to complete the frame, first from the center and then around the middle.

4 Finally, the spider fills in the frame with stretchy silk. It bites and kills insects caught in its sticky trap.

 INSECT TRAPS

Here's a way to trap insects so that you can study them without harming them.

1 Bury a glass jar outdoors. Place a lid on stones, to keep rain from filling the jar.

2 Check your trap every morning to see what you've caught. Try to find the insects' names in a guide book, then let them go.

3 Put traps in wet places and dry places, to see whether you catch the same kinds of creatures in each habitat.

Are spiders insects?

Although you might think spiders look like beetles and other crawling insects, they belong to a separate animal group called the arachnids. The main difference between the two groups is that insects have six legs, while arachnids, such as spiders and scorpions, have eight.

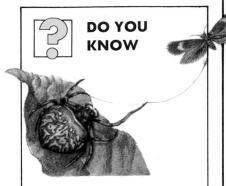
INSECT FACTS

• Experts have named over 850,000 insects. Another 7,000 or so are named every year.

• Dragonflies are fast fliers – they have been recorded reaching speeds of 49 mph!

• Butterflies and moths feed on the nectar of flowers, sipping it through special mouth-parts called proboscises.

• Both ants and bees live in large groups called colonies.

• Flies have one pair of flying wings. Their knobby back wings help with balance.

• Beetles have hard cases to cover and protect their wings. This is a stag beetle.

• Bugs range in size from tiny aphids $\frac{1}{10}$ inch long (above) to giants of $4\frac{1}{2}$ inches!

• Grasshoppers are jumpers, with strong back legs. They fly with their back wings.

How do bees make honey?

Bees make honey from pollen and nectar, which they collect from flowers in summer. Back at their hive, the bees put the mixture into little wax "rooms" called cells. The cells are six-sided and join to make the shape we call a honeycomb. The bees make a special substance in their bodies which they add to the mixture. This turns it into honey for them to eat in winter.

 BEE FACTS

● Large beehives may have 60,000 worker bees in them, but only one queen.

● It takes the life's work of 10 bees to fill one 16-ounce pot of honey.

Bees store pollen and nectar in wax honey-combs, where it turns into honey.

 TEST INSECT TASTES

Try this outdoors on a warm day when there are lots of insects about. Ask a grownup to help you, and don't get too close, as some insects will sting if disturbed. You'll need four dishes and some colored paper.

1 Stand each dish on a square of colored paper. Put milk in one dish, sugary water in the 2nd, salty water in the 3rd, and jam in the 4th. Label the paper for each different food.

2 Wait to see which insects come to feed. Note which ones visit each dish. Count how many insects feed in half an hour, and see which food attracts the most insects to it.

Sugar   Salt   Jam   Milk

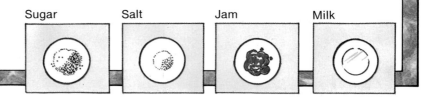

Why do bees and wasps sting?

Bees and wasps sting for different reasons. A worker bee stings to defend its hive. It can use its sting only once, then it dies. Queen bees fight each other, though, and can sting more than once. Wasps can also sting several times. They use their stings to stun or kill other insects.

A bee sting (below) is a barbed tube, which hooks tightly in place while poison is pumped down it.

How do flies walk upside down?

Flies have special hooks and sucker pads on their feet (left) which help them walk upside down.

Flies can walk up windows and across ceilings because they have special hooks and sucker pads on their feet instead of toes. These can grip even the smoothest surface. Houseflies like the insect above have two hooked claws and two sticky sucker pads on each foot.

 **DO YOU KNOW**

The buzzing of a fly is the sound of its wings beating at over 100 times a second.

When did dinosaurs live?

None of our human ancestors ever saw a live dinosaur. This is because dinosaurs died out 65 million years ago, long before human beings appeared on Earth. We have learned about dinosaurs by studying their fossils – bones and other body remains which over the centuries have turned to stone. This is how we know that the dinosaur age started 225 million years ago and continued for about 160 million years.

The pterosaurs weren't dinosaurs, but they lived at the same time. They also died out about 65 million years ago.

Corythosaurus was a plant-eating dinosaur, about 32 feet long, with a ducklike bill and a crest on its head.

Brachiosaurus was a gigantic 75 feet long! Its long neck helped it to browse at the top of the tallest plants.

Stegosaurus moved slowly but was heavily armored, with bony plates on its back and a spiked tail.

DO YOU KNOW

Dinosaur fossils have been found which show that some dinosaurs were even larger than Brachiosaurus. Called Ultrasaurus, these super-dinosaurs were 115 feet long and could easily have peered over our rooftops!

Tyrannosaurus was one of the largest meat eaters ever. It was 50 feet long and had large sharp teeth up to 7 inches long.

Ornitholestes was the size of a dog. It was a meat-eating hunter and could run swiftly on its long back legs.

Triceratops was about 29 feet long. It had a huge armored head, with three horns for fighting off enemies.

Why do animals become extinct?

One of the main reasons why animals become extinct, or die out, is because a major change takes place in their habitat – the weather becomes too cold or too hot, for example, or the plants or animals on which they feed are hard to find. Nowadays, these changes are often brought about by people. Even bulldozing a small forest to make way for new houses can cause some of the animals that lived there to become extinct.

The survival of the gentle gorilla is now threatened, as more and more of its forest habitat is destroyed.

DANGER FACTS

● More than 300 bird and mammal species have died out since the 1600s. In that time, the number of human beings has increased from 450 million to over 5 billion.

● Thousands of animals are now on the danger list – from tiny insects like the butterfly below, to giants like the African elephant and the blue whale.

Regal fritillary

Javan rhino

● There are fewer than 50 Javan rhinos left in the world.

● Experts think that unless habitats are protected, we may lose as many as 15 mammal, 30 bird, 90 fish, and 2,000 insect species every single year.

Useful words

Amphibian One of the main groups of vertebrate animals. Amphibians live on land and in water, and they include frogs and toads, salamanders and newts. Most amphibians have damp, slimy skin and lay jelly-like eggs.

Backbone Another word for spine – the row of bones which runs down the back of humans and all other vertebrate animals.

Gill A body part for breathing oxygen from water. Fish have gills for breathing underwater.

Habitat The area surrounding an animal's home. It includes the weather and the plants that grow there, as well as the other animals that live there.

Hibernation A type of deep sleep which can last several months. Some animals hibernate when there is very little food or water around, or when the weather is very cold. During this time the animals hardly ever wake up and they don't eat. Instead, they live off their own body fat.

Fly   Butterfly   Bee

Invertebrate An animal which doesn't have a backbone. Jellyfish, worms, and insects such as flies and bees are all invertebrates. Some invertebrates, such as snails, have an outside shell to protect their soft bodies. There are over 1 million invertebrate species.

Lung A body part for breathing oxygen from air. All mammals have lungs – even whales!

Mammal An animal that feeds its young on milk from the mother's body. Mammals have lungs for breathing air.

Marsupial A type of mammal which raises its young in the mother's pouch. Kangaroos are marsupials, for example.

Reptile One of the main groups of vertebrate animals. Snakes and lizards, crocodiles and alligators, turtles and tortoises are all reptiles. Unlike fish and amphibians, with their slimy skin and jelly-like eggs, most reptiles have dry, scaly skin and the eggs they lay have leathery skins.

Species A unique or special type of animal. Blue whales are one species within the whale group, for example. Other whale species are humpback whales and sperm whales.

Vertebrate An animal with a backbone. The main groups of vertebrates are fish, amphibians, reptiles, birds, and mammals. There are about 45,000 vertebrate species.

Index